Praise for *Fi*

"As a screenwriter and self-published author, I've always sought ... .'s help with my loglines. Having read this book I can testify it contains all his best advice and provides a lighthearted but thorough crash course to loglines. If more writers would heed the advice on these pages, they would avoid the inept pitches and synopses so common among self-published authors. Highly recommended as an essential read for any writer."

Aubrey Hansen, author and screenwriter
http://www.aubreyhansen.com

"Whether you are traditionally published or have hopped aboard the self-published train, you need to do all you can to help market your book. Finding the Core of Your Story should be required reading for all who have written books and want them noticed. I did not know what a logline was until I read this book, now I realize how vital this little one line (or two or three) is. Jordan Smith gives us the benefits of his experience with both humor and integral advice on how to write the best logline for your book. This is a must read for all authors!"

LA Ramsey, author and novelist
http://laramsey.com

"Not only was the book extremely helpful and well laid out, but it was incredibly fun to read! The author is personable and down-to-earth and had me laughing several times. With this book, you are just a short, enjoyable read away from creating your own masterful logline."

J. Grace Pennington, author of *Firmament: Radialloy* and *Never*
http://jgracepennington.com

"Jordan has a way of presenting his tips and tricks without getting bogged down in details, leaving readers with no doubt as to what he was trying to say. This method of precise communication enables storytellers to improve their own writing without having to struggle through understanding what was just conveyed to them."

Katie Lynn Daniels, author of the *Supervillain of the Day* series
http://katielynndaniels.com

"As an aspiring author with two books in progress, it is really easy to get bogged down in minute details and the inflections/tone of each scene or chapter. This book helped me to take a step back and look at the big picture."

Jo M. Coleman
http://jomcoleman.com

"I read this neat little book in a matter of hours, highlighting something from almost every chapter for later reference. It was enjoyable and easy to read, while teaching me a lot about story. If you're writing a story, planning one out, or wrote one in the past, you need this book."

Jeremiah Stiles
http://www.another-otherworld.com

Finding the Core of Your Story

How to strengthen and sell your story in one essential sentence

By Jordan Smith

Cover design by John Shafer

ISBN: 1481045407
ISBN-13: 978-1481045407

To everyone who believed I could

The Stuff Inside This Book

Introduction   9

So, What Is a Logline in the First Place?   13

The Quick-Start Logline Chapter   19

Untangling the Threads of Your Story   27

You've Gotta Promise Me Something   33

It's a Must to be Forced   37

Tickle Me with Your Adjective Feather   41

Stop Avoiding Conflict   47

How Ironic That We Don't Use Irony   53

Do You Ever Feel Set Up?   59

What Makes Your Story Different?   63

Leave the Moral Out of This!   67

The Handy-Dandy Three-Sentence Trick   73

Characters Deserve Loglines Too   79

In a World Where…   85

Finding the Core of Your Series   91

I Wrote a Logline… Now What?   99

Acknowledgments   105

Who Wrote This Book, Anyways?   107

Introduction

Let's say you and I get onto an elevator together and I ask what your story is about. You could do one of two things.

You could start from the beginning and try to pitch me your entire 300-page novel or two-hour film in the brief elevator ride. If you take this approach, you'll probably be eyeing the emergency stop button as the elevator gets closer and closer to my floor while you haven't even gotten to the story's hook yet. But, alas, you're too late. We arrive at my floor and I get off rolling my eyes and wondering why I asked.

Or, instead of trying to pitch your entire movie in such a short time, you could just give me one sentence that succinctly summarizes your story's hook and key ingredients. In the time that it takes to ride an elevator, you've hopefully tickled my fancy enough for me to give you my e-mail address and say, "I've gotta run now, but send me some more about this, okay?"

That one sentence you gave me is called a *logline*. It's a tool that originated in Hollywood and is used by screenwriters to pitch their screenplays to movie producers. Basically, it's a one-sentence summary of your story.

But you don't need to be a screenwriter to use loglines. In fact, I think you're seriously shooting yourself in the foot if you don't use them. For too long, though, the logline has been stuck almost exclusively in the realm of screenwriters, and that's a shame. It's not just a screenwriting tool; any storyteller can use it. It doesn't matter if you write novels, movies, plays, comic books, video games, or even operas. Every storyteller should be able to say in one sentence what his story is about, and this book is designed to teach you to do just that.

Now, you'll notice that the examples I use in this book are largely from movies, and that's because my story medium of choice is screenwriting. Just remember, you can use loglines for any kind of story you like to write.

You might be wondering, though, why you need to be able to write a logline. Well, a logline is a way for you to do a few things:

- You'll be able to pitch your story quickly and compellingly. No more fumbling for words when somebody asks you what your story is about!

- You'll have a guide to make sure your story is on the right track. Handy for shaping the next revision, whether it's draft 2 or draft 17.

- You'll even be able to solve story issues before they start if you write a logline before you get too far into the writing process. Solve your story issues in draft 1 and save yourself some trouble later.

Sounds good, doesn't it? A logline is a very valuable tool, and you can get off and running with these little gems by simply continuing to read this book.

Okay, that's great! But why should I listen to you?

That's a fair question. Here's a little about me and my logline journey.

I learned about loglines through a contest on a filmmaking forum I frequent. That got me hooked on these things, and I've been studying them ever since. As I've helped a good number of members improve their loglines, I've gained a reputation on the forum as the logline guru, and I was even chosen to help judge our second logline contest.

As I helped people with loglines, I started to notice patterns, so I began putting together some basic logline rules. To share these rules, I posted a series of articles on my blog about how to write a great logline.

The response to my blog series was huge. Storytellers contacted me and told me how useful the information was. That blog series was only a partial look at loglines, though. There was a whole lot more I could add to the tips in my blog posts, so I wrote this book to put it all in one place.

And I think we're all set to head into logline world, so please follow me to the first chapter.

So, What Is a Logline in the First Place?

It's always important to start with a good definition, so let me explain what a logline is and some of the conventions of using one.

Let's start with the name. Who came up with that crazy *logline* thing, anyway?

As far as I can make out, the term *logline* (or *log line,* as some people insist on writing it) originated in early Hollywood. Studios would stack scripts in vaults, which made it tough to figure out what was what without disturbing the whole pile.

To counter this calamity, some brilliant person came up with the idea of sticking a one-line summary onto the spine of the script. That way, you could read the loglines and quickly find the one you wanted.

Now we have digital screenplays, so loglines are a different kind of shortcut. Film professionals are busy busy busy people. They don't have the time of day to read all the screenplays that come across their desks, so they read the loglines instead. If one grabs them, they might just read the script. Maybe. If their coffee isn't too cold.

"Okay, that makes sense," you say, "but I write novels, not

movies. I don't need to convince a film professional to buy my screenplay."

You've just hit upon one of my pet peeves about loglines. Nobody outside of filmmaking seems to know about this powerful tool. And that's a shame, because you can use it no matter what you're writing. You may not have to pitch to a producer, but you will have to sell agents, publishers, illustrators, and readers on your masterpiece. So forget what medium you're telling your story in. Just write a logline, okay?

Now. I didn't know the interesting origin of the term *logline* until I began to write this chapter. Along the way, I discovered something else. Something terrible.

There are things called loglines out there that are not loglines! Or at the very least, they aren't good loglines.

It seems that the people who write TV Guide and the descriptions for DVR listings have twisted the beautiful form of this indispensable device and made it something laughable. Really, go to movies.tvguide.com, skim some of these disasters that they claim are loglines, and you tell me if any of them are really compelling.

They tend to look something like this:

Megamind: Tom McGrath directed this animated comedy about a super villain who wants to try being the good guy. Will Ferrell stars as the title character.

The Adventures of Tintin: Jamie Bell is joined by Andy Serkis in this action adventure film which marks director Steven Spielberg's animation film debut. Daniel Craig is brilliant as the villain Sakharine.

Those are not real loglines. And that brings us to a discussion of what a logline is.

Jordan Smith

A logline is a way to break your story down to its lowest common denominator. It's a sentence that tells what the story is at its core. You're trying to write the elevator statement version of your story.

what's an elevator statement?

"Got it," you say. "But what's an elevator statement?"

Remember our little elevator scene in the introduction? <u>An elevator statement is a pitch that's short enough to give someone in an elevator.</u>

Powerful, ain't it? If you already knew about loglines, you're probably cackling like a villain with a destruct-o ray.

But can you do anything with a logline besides hit me with it on an elevator ride?

Of course you can! *What can loglines be used for?*

A logline is like that great actor who never gets typecast. It's versatile and can play more than one role. Not only can you use it to <u>tell somebody what your story is about</u>, but you can also use it to tell *yourself* <u>what your story is about.</u>

"But I know what my story is about!" you protest.

Really? Can you tell me in one sentence?

Crickets chirp

That's what I thought.

If you don't know what your story is about in a single sentence, you run the risk of meandering your story into places where it doesn't belong. You fall into the trap of putting everything and the kitchen sink in because you don't know what your story is. (Though the latter is not usually admitted and often materializes with the excuse of, "But it's cool!")

By the way, while we're on the topic of single sentences, let me just square something away real quick. A lot of people quibble over the length of these amazing storytelling tools. There are those who will tell you that a logline can have two sentences (I've even seen people say it's three.), but I am a very firm believer in the single-sentence logline. It's neater, it looks less intimidating, and it forces you to condense things into as small a space as possible. And that means it's easier to memorize your logline for that mythical elevator moment.

There's another neat thing you can do with a logline. You can use it as a basis for marketing materials.

Once you know the core essence of your story, you can take your handy single-sentence logline and expand it with more details to create all sorts of things—things like a summary or the blurb on the back cover. And we'll cover that in more detail at the end of this adventure, so stay tuned!

At this point, I hope I've convinced you that you're going to want to get your story into a logline before you write "FADE IN" or "It was a dark and stormy night." Tape it to your monitor (or typewriter if you're still in the dark ages) if you have to. Remember, you're promising us something with this story. Find your story's core and tell us your premise in a single sentence, then make us happy by sticking to it and delivering on your promise.

And if you've already written a draft or three, that's okay! Just decide not to write another draft until you can boil your story down to a logline. Your next draft will thank you. (It might even send you a card! Wait, what? Your drafts don't do that?)

Just so you know, you generally format a logline like this:

TITLE: My Great Movie

GENRE: Drama

LOGLINE: This is my logline.

For the purposes of this book, however, I'm going to write loglines like this:

My Great Movie: This is my logline.

And that's just because I think it looks neater. The reason you include the longer format is really for the genre section. Sometimes including the genre can make your audience think in a certain direction. But we're here for the loglines, so I'll be condensing the format.

How this book works

First, we'll jump right into the world of loglines in the very next chapter, which is a handy-dandy crash-course in logline building. Then, we'll take a look at the components of a logline and cover each in detail, rubbing our hands together with glee over the power of what we're learning. Once we're done there, we'll deal with some common pitfalls one by one.

You'll also find some exercises at the end of each chapter. Personally, I never do these things, but some people like exercises, so I threw them in just in case somebody wanted some to do. Your choice.

Let's start writing a great logline. This should be fun!

The Quick-Start Logline Chapter

This chapter is designed to get you going really, really fast. Like, by the time you get to the end of the chapter, you should be able to write a fairly decent logline. What I'm going to do is show you a couple of logline templates and then go over what I consider to be the fundamental logline rules. So let's jump right in!

If you were to write a logline with placeholders for each of the story elements, the most basic logline might look something like this:

Logline Template 1

An adjective protagonist must do something that will set up a climactic encounter with an adjective antagonist/antagonistic force.

Some loglines are a bit more complicated than that, and we'll get there in a minute (depending on how fast you read!), but let's break this one down for now.

What four things must every logline contain?

Every logline needs to contain four things:

1. A protagonist

2. The situation

3. The protagonist's goal

4. An antagonist

(In case you were sleeping during vocabulary class, the protagonist is your main character, and the antagonist is the person or force that opposes him. If you knew that before now, pat yourself on the back and feel free to look superior.)

That's a story in its most basic form, and you'll see all of those elements from the above template in every completed logline in this book and in every good story (and most halfway-decent ones) you come across. Sometimes it's subtle, sometimes it's blatant, but those are always there. If you're missing one... Well, you don't have a story yet.

Don't contradict me. Just put this book away and find those four things in your story, then come back. The rest of you follow me. This next part is cool.

The Four Fundamental Logline Rules

As I've helped people write loglines, I've run into some common errors. So you can avoid such mistakes, I've put together four fundamental logline rules for you to follow (ain't I sweet?).

Fundamental Logline Rule #1: Always tell us about your main characters in a simple adjective-noun pair.

It's really easy and lots of fun to do this part. Take your protagonist and come up with a noun for him, like one of these:

- Policeman

- Teenager

- Chef

Then brainstorm some adjectives that describe him, like this:

- Happy-go-lucky
- Ginormous
- Crafty

Put 'em together and you get your adjective-noun pair, like this:

- Happy-go-lucky policeman
- Ginormous teenager
- Crafty chef

Simple, right? Fun, right? I could do this all day. But we have loglines to write.

You can do the same thing for the antagonist or antagonistic force. Show us who he is and why he's bad in that little pair. And yes, you should probably stay away from clichés like "world-dominating overlord." *what should you do when antagonistic force is a natural disaster?*

This can get a little tricky when you have an antagonistic force like a hurricane or something like that, because it's pretty hard to make a hurricane more scary. So usually, natural disasters are compelling enough in themselves. After all, you're not going to find much of an audience for a story about The Tsunami That Was So Threatening It Didn't Kill Anybody.

what's a antagonistic force

By the way, in case you're wondering, an *antagonistic force* is a non-personal source of antagonism. That is, in stories where you don't have a person playing the role of the villain, something else takes its place. As above, it could be a force of nature or some other life problem, such as going into debt or the threat of starvation.

The second rule goes with the protagonist and antagonist, so let's cover that now.

Fundamental Logline Rule #2: Don't name names.

We're interested in the essence of your story, not the names of your characters. Your character's name doesn't tell us anything about him, so don't use it. Same with made-up cities, countries, etc.

There's one exception to this, and that's actual historical figures or people from existing works of fiction. Ulysses S. Grant, Robin Hood, the Wizard of Oz. Long story short, if you're writing a logline for *Wicked*, you definitely need to mention the Wicked Witch of the West.

And yes, real places can be named. Rule of thumb, though: Don't. Unless you really have to. But generally, you can write a compelling logline without telling us where the story is set.

Fundamental Logline Rule #3: Keep it simple.

This means that we're looking for the very core of the story (have you been getting that vibe?), so anything not important to the main thread of your story should be saved for your summary, where you have more room to flesh things out. Subplots and extraneous phrasing must all be chopped out without mercy.

A quick word on extraneous phrases. There are many sorts of these things, so I'll give a couple of examples just to get your wheels turning in the right direction.

First, I once told someone that the phrase "sets off in the dark of night" was too pretty for a logline. Why? We're trying to get the essence here. You can use those pretty phrases in the back copy. For now, just tell us the main event.

Second, there are phrases like "in order to" and "so that he can" that can easily be trimmed down to "to" and "so he can," respectively. Break out those scissors and cut those large phrases down to size.

Fundamental Logline Rule #4: Show us the conflict.

Notice our logline structure. Something is opposing our protagonist. This is conflict.

If you don't have conflict, you don't have story. Every good logline shows compelling conflict, whether internal or external. Get it in there.

(And I know this last rule is short. That's because <u>conflict is the core of story</u> and it takes a while to discuss properly. The above is the ultra-condensed version and we'll get to an entire chapter on it later.)

So there you have the four fundamental logline rules. You can write a logline!

Oh, wait. Hold your horses a minute. I told you there was another logline template to come. Let's cover that now.

Sometimes, your story will need some setup to logline nicely. When you have one like that, you might need a slightly different version of the handy-dandy logline template. Something more like this.

Logline Template 2

After something happens to set things up, an adjective protagonist must do something that will set up a climactic encounter with an adjective antagonist/antagonistic force.

I call that opening part "the setup clause." Basically, you include a phrase that will set up the rest of the logline with some key information. It's kind of difficult to explain in a short space, so I have an example coming. Hold on a second! I've also devoted an entire chapter to it later in the book.

In fact, this whole chapter is just the basics. It's enough to get you off and running with your own loglines. Pretty much everything I've talked about here will be covered in greater detail as you read on. (How's that for an incentive?)

You're pretty much all set to write your own logline. But first, because it often helps to see things in practice, here are example loglines I've written for two movies that you might have seen.

National Treasure: A daring treasure hunter's next clue is on the back of the Declaration of Independence, which he must steal to keep it safe from a ruthless rival.

This one uses Logline Template 1. We have a protagonist (a daring treasure hunter), who must do something (steal the Declaration of Independence), which sets up a climactic encounter with an antagonist (he'll have to meet and overcome the ruthless rival before the movie ends).

Bolt: After he is mistakenly shipped to New York, a TV-star dog who thinks he's a superhero must survive the real world to get back to his owner in Hollywood.

This one uses Logline Template 2. We have a setup (after he is mistakenly shipped to New York), a protagonist (a TV-star dog), who must do something (survive the real world), to set up a climactic encounter with an antagonist (the real world is the antagonist, which must be survived to get to the climax of reunion with his owner).

You can see how these templates are very loose and flexible. I really hope you don't try to write a logline that fits one of them exactly, because these are not formulas to be followed strictly. Instead, I want you to flex the templates and use them as a reminder of the components of a logline.

The goal here is for you to understand what you need to tell me about your story for me to get the idea. Once you have those elements down, you can play with the format all you like. Don't let the tools be your master; master the tools.

We're just getting started here, so check out the exercises below, and then read on for more adventures in the land of loglines.

Exercises

- Pick a book or movie that you really like. Write a logline for it using the templates from this chapter.

- Now that you have a basic idea of logline structure, take a story you're working on and write a logline for it.

(Oh yeah... Feel free to do these out of order if you find one easier than the other. There's a reason I didn't number them!)

Untangling the Threads of Your Story

Oftentimes when you meet a beginning storyteller and ask what he's writing, he'll give you a logline that goes something like this:

My Great Movie: While the main character is working hard at his job, something big happens, causing him to go on a journey to defeat his inner darkness so he can confront the evil in the city around him, all while he tries to reconcile with his estranged parents and get the perfect girl to fall for him.

The problem here is that the writer can't find the main story thread. And chances are good that you're having the same problem. Let's take a look at a Hollywood film and see how this plays out.

Here's what happens when we take *Jurassic Park* and write a logline that follows the above pattern:

Jurassic Park: When a dinosaur park goes haywire and the monsters get loose, a kid-hating scientist must protect two children while another group of scientists tries to fix the park before everyone gets eaten.

Now we're getting our A-story and B-story mixed up. But wait! What do I mean by A-story and B-story? Let's define those terms first.

What is A-story and B-story?

An *A-story* is the main thread of the story. It's the main reason we came to see this movie, or decided to read this book, or whatever medium the story is in.

The *B-story* is something on the side that supplements and informs the A-story, often by showing the flip side of the theme, but it plays second fiddle to the main thread of the A-story.

And you're not limited to two stories. You can have as many as you need (which is not the same as having as many as you want). This is especially easy to pick up on with something like the *Lord of the Rings* trilogy, as our heroes end up splitting into three distinct groups, along with several other threads running throughout that epic three-part story.

The key here is to find the main thrust of your story and keep the logline about that story only. This requires that you actually know what your story is about! (Now there's a concept.)

At its core, *Jurassic Park* is about how the scientist and the kids bond while avoiding the Tyrannosaurus Rex and her raptor buddies. The part about fixing the park is secondary. Our main group of the scientist and the kids could escape being lunch in any number of ways. It's not dependent on the park getting fixed, though that'd sure be nice!

Because the scientist and the kids are the focus of the story, we can take out the part about fixing the park, boiling this logline down to a single A-story thread.

Jurassic Park: A kid-hating scientist must protect two children when a dinosaur park goes haywire and the monsters go on rampage.

"But wait!" you say. "My movie is much more complicated than *Jurassic Park*! I have more than one main character, and I'm following multiple story threads that get really tangled up. I

28

can't boil this down to a main thread because I can't pull one thread without the rest coming along like so much spaghetti!"

I hear you. Let's write a logline for a movie with lots of story threads. And let's make it harder by picking one with multiple main characters.

Pirates of the Caribbean – The Curse of the Black Pearl: A band of cursed pirates attempts to lift the curse by kidnapping the governor's daughter, which sends her brave lover hot on the pirates' heels with a pirate captain out for revenge on his former crew, but both ships are pursued by the daughter's jealous and pirate-hating suitor.

Whew! That's a lot to work over! (And it's quite the run-on sentence into the bargain, not to mention that monster of a title making the logline look even longer!) We have lots of story threads to follow here, so let's break them down.

- The story of the lover (Will) and pirate captain (Jack) trying to catch the pirates.

- The story of the rival suitor (Captain Norrington) trying to catch the pirates and Will and Jack.

- The story of the love triangle between Elizabeth, Will, and Norrington.

- The story of the pirates trying to lift the curse. *1*

- The story of Jack's revenge plot. *2.*

But which one of those five stories is the main thread in this complicated film? Often with these types of films, you can look for the character with the largest arc or the character with the epilogue moment, but here that's just not the case. Though the story seems to follow Elizabeth, Will has the biggest arc, and Jack gets the epilogue (drink up, me hearties, yo ho!), so that's not going to work here.

What we can do, in this case, is boil the movie down to the main thread that ties everything else together. For *Pirates*, it's the chase to save Elizabeth, regardless of which of the three ships we're following at a given moment. If we run with that idea, we get a logline more like this:

Pirates of the Caribbean – Curse of the Black Pearl: When the governor's daughter is captured by pirates, her brave lover must join forces with a half-mad pirate captain to save her.

Okay, that's much better, but it's not too compelling. How is this movie different from all the other swashbuckling-and-pirates-on-the-high-seas movies? We could add a bit about the curse to really amp this up and show the uniqueness of the story:

Pirates of the Caribbean – Curse of the Black Pearl: When the governor's daughter is kidnapped by a band of cursed pirates, her brave lover must join forces with a half-mad pirate captain to save her before she is sacrificed to end the curse.

Now we have higher stakes, so this version shows more of the excitement. We also see that this is a curse-lifting voyage and not a treasure hunt, which is even more interesting!

If we wanted another take on this logline, we could try playing up Jack's strained relationship with his old crew.

Pirates of the Caribbean – Curse of the Black Pearl: When the governor's daughter is kidnapped by a band of cursed pirates, her brave lover must join forces with the only man who can help him save her – the half-mad former captain of the cursed crew.

Either of those last two versions could work, depending on which angle you want to approach the story from. But remember, the logline is meant to grab the audience and make them ask for more, so you want to give them the version that is the most compelling, then feed them the other details after they show interest.

Personally, I'd go with the version that plays up the curse. And if Wikipedia is to be believed, that's the angle that sold the screenplay, so it's probably not a bad choice!

Exercises

- Pick a book or movie that has a lot of story threads. Try to find the A-story and write a logline for that story.

- Does your story's logline need its threads untangled? List all of the stories in your story and pick out the A-story, then write your logline to emphasize it.

You've Gotta Promise Me Something

As we've already seen in the previous two chapters, loglines are pretty powerful. But there's a catch to writing a good one: you have to promise me something.

A lot of people will make their loglines vague. This usually stems from one of a few problems.

- The writer doesn't have a core to his story.

- The writer doesn't want to give too much away.

- The writer is trying to put too much of the scope of his epic story into too small a space.

All three of these tend to produce loglines like this:

My Great Movie: A hero must defeat the darkness within himself before he can conquer the darkness in the world around him.

Let's take a few movies and see what happens when we use that formula to write a logline, shall we?

Jurassic Park: A scientist must defeat the darkness within himself before he can defeat the darkness outside.

Facing the Giants: A coach and his football team must defeat the darkness within themselves before they can defeat the darkness outside.

The Chronicles of Narnia – The Voyage of the Dawn Treader: A boatload of adventurers must defeat the darkness within themselves before they can defeat the darkness outside.

Would you go see any of these movies with descriptions like that? Okay, maybe *Narnia*… I sure did! But that example aside, you need to tell us what makes your story different from all of those others, so give us some plot details.

When we talk about inner and outer darkness, we're really trying to convey the conflict in the story. Conflict can come from inside (the darkness within yourself) or from an external source.

For example, if a character is struggling with anger issues, that's internal darkness. But if the character is, say, Luke Skywalker struggling against Darth Vader, now you have external darkness.

Defining the darkness always makes things more interesting. Watch what happens when we tell what the darkness actually is in the loglines from before.

Jurassic Park: A kid-hating scientist must protect two children when a dinosaur park goes haywire and the monsters go on rampage.

Facing the Giants: A failing coach and his terrible football team transform their game by playing football for God rather than men.

The Chronicles of Narnia – The Voyage of the Dawn Treader: A boatload of adventurers must defeat the darkness within themselves before they can defeat the darkness outside.

(Oops, that one didn't have much else for plot. Seriously, I think that was the real logline for the film! But it's still a fun movie and it makes me cry, so we'll forgive it.)

Do you see how much more compelling these loglines are when we name the inner darkness? What's even better is if you can also tell us what the outer darkness is, as in the logline from *Jurassic Park*. Label the darknesses (*flaws* or *problems* would be better words) with some imagination-tickling adjectives. Make us see the possibilities of the story in that single sentence. To borrow from Blake Snyder's excellent book *Save the Cat!*, you need to promise us the premise.

why does a logline exist?

Remember, a logline exists to plant an idea in the mind of the audience. (Sorry, I just went all *Inception* on you.) A well-written logline will spark the intended audience into imagining all the possibilities of what could happen in Act 2 (or the middle of the film, if you don't believe in acts), where the real fun of the story takes place, or as *Save the Cat!* puts it so well, during the Fun and Games section of the movie.

So in your logline, make me see how fun or interesting your story could be. Of the above examples, *Jurassic Park* does the best job. You can see not only the threat of the dinosaurs, but you can also see that this character will have to change his mind about kids if they want to escape being raptor food. It's also the best-developed story of the three. Coincidence? I think not!

You're going to find as you work on this skill that an epic-sized idea (especially a series of books) is probably the hardest to do this with. But keep at it. If you've really got something good, you should be able to boil it down to a single sentence. Your audience will thank you for it.

Exercises

- Pick some of your favorite stories and list the specific darknesses that must be defeated in each one. Then write a logline for one or two and name the darknesses.

- Does your story's logline promise something? Find out what you can promise in your story and make sure that goes into your logline.

It's a Must to be Forced

Now that we've spent a few chapters talking about the biggest logline woes, I want to share a tip that can often punch up a good logline and make it great.

It's the simple use of either the word *must* or *forced*. Let's look at some loglines to see how these small words can be used in a powerful way.

In the last chapter, I gave a few loglines for existing movies that I had written as examples. First, I want to come back to the best example from last time, which was the logline for *Jurassic Park*. Let's write that logline two ways.

Version 1: *Jurassic Park*: A kid-hating scientist protects two children when a dinosaur park goes haywire and the monsters go on rampage.

Version 2: *Jurassic Park*: A kid-hating scientist must protect two children when a dinosaur park goes haywire and the monsters go on rampage.

Which one is more compelling? The second version. But why?

The only difference between those two loglines is the word *must*. That one word implies so much extra that just isn't there in the first version. It means this guy is thrown into a situation where he has to do something he hates. It means we're going to see him stretch and change for better or worse. It means he didn't exactly make the decision to protect the kids on his own, which means conflict, and conflict is story. Will he change his attitude toward the kids, or will he end up abandoning them?

By implying all of that with one small word, we've suddenly made this logline much more interesting. Let's see if we can apply this trick to my logline for *Facing the Giants*, which could use some extra oomph. Here's what we had last time:

Facing the Giants: A failing coach and his terrible football team transform their game by playing football for God rather than men.

To get this one to a point where we can use our trick, we're going to need to do a little bit of rewriting. We'll use Logline Template #2 to rewrite it to look like this:

> *Facing the Giants*: Faced with losing his job, a failing coach must rally his pitiful team to transform their game by playing football for God rather than men.

As with the *Jurassic Park* example, this one is improved by including the word *must*, but there's a little more going on here. In the original logline, we had nothing that would have forced the coach to change. We had to fix that before we could use our trick, so we added the opening setup clause, "Faced with losing his job," to set up the conflict before dropping our magic word. Now we have a much more compelling logline!

When you've gotten pretty good at using *must*, you can start using the *forced*. (You know you saw that bad *Star Wars* joke coming.) It works on the same principle, but with one caveat. You have to make sure that you use *forced* only when it's appropriate.

Because the word *forced* implies that our hero has no choice or is thrown into a situation, make sure that he has no other option before you exchange *must* for *forced*. It wouldn't be appropriate to use in our *Jurassic Park* logline, since our scientist could have run away and left the kids to themselves, and we'd still have had a story to tell. But what if we were writing a logline for a movie like *Apollo 13*?

Apollo 13: When a moon mission goes terribly wrong, three astronauts are forced to improvise a new way home.

You could use *must* here, but *forced* works well in this case because the astronauts are thrown into this situation with no immediate way out except to give up right now and die. And since we certainly wouldn't come to the theater to see that (or I wouldn't have, anyway), we know that the astronauts have been forced to come up with a way home.

Try this with your own loglines and see what wonders a *must* or *forced* can work. While this trick isn't for every logline, and you can write a good one without adding either of these words, one of these handy little words might be just what you need to add some extra punch.

Exercises

- Go stare at your movie or book shelf and decide which stories would use *must* and which would use *forced* in a logline. Bonus points if you reorganize the shelf to sort your books or movies by that criteria!

- Can you improve your logline with a *must* or *forced*? Remember that this doesn't work for every story, but it never hurts to try!

Tickle Me with Your Adjective Feather

A key component of a great logline is a good, solid adjective. You remember adjectives from grammar class, right? They're those descriptive words that go before nouns to give color to a sentence and help you form a mental picture of the person, place, or thing.

Let's take some rather bland Hollywood movie loglines and see what we can do with adjectives to improve them. We'll do two films from previous chapters, and we'll also do a new one so you can see the process a little better.

Jurassic Park: A scientist must protect two children when a dinosaur park goes haywire and the monsters go on rampage.

Pirates of the Caribbean – Curse of the Black Pearl: When the governor's daughter is kidnapped by a band of pirates, her lover must join forces with a pirate captain to save her before she is sacrificed to end a curse.

How to Train Your Dragon: Against the traditions of his Viking tribe, a boy befriends a dragon and discovers secrets about the creatures that will change his tribe's way of life forever.

All of these loglines are missing a key ingredient. We need to describe any characters mentioned in the logline with a good, imagination-tickling adjective. What we're after here is a descriptive word that gives our reader a feel for who each character is. Let's jump in and take it from the top.

For our *Jurassic Park* logline, we have to describe the scientist. To find our adjective, we can make a list of words that could describe him.

- Adventurous
- Tall
- Kid-hating
- Rough
- Computer-breaking

You've read the previous chapters, so you ought to know that I'm going to pick *kid-hating* from this list. That's because it sets up the conflict and irony of the situation better than the other choices.

Jurassic Park: A kid-hating scientist must protect two children when a dinosaur park goes haywire and the monsters go on rampage.

Okay, that one was pretty easy. We only needed to describe one character. We could try giving the children an adjective, but it's not going to add any necessary information about the story, so we're done.

Let's try *Pirates of the Caribbean*, where we need to describe a bunch of characters. We need adjectives for the pirates, the lover, and the pirate captain. (We could also do the daughter, but the three characters I've selected are the important ones that make this logline work, so we'll leave her out of the adjective-ing.)

Let's brainstorm for the pirates.

- Angry
- Cursed
- Smelly
- Flea-bitten
- Undead

Undead could work here, but since we bring in the curse later, let's use *cursed* to set it up so that it doesn't come out of nowhere at the end of the logline.

Now let's do the lover.

- Scrupulous
- Brave
- Blacksmith
- Legolas-look-alike
- Lovestruck

Much as I'd like to go with *Legolas-look-alike*, that's not going to work here. *Lovestruck* is just redundant (I was groping for adjectives, can't you tell?), and *blacksmith* tells us nothing about the character. I used *brave* in a previous chapter, but I'm going to go with *scrupulous* this time. Again, it plays to the irony of this upright young man joining up with a pirate captain to get the job done. And speaking of the pirate captain...

- Tipsy
- Perpetually drunk
- Half-mad
- Carefree
- Untrustworthy

I struggled with which of these to use when I wrote this logline, but I settled on *half-mad* because the character is portrayed as somewhat not all there. Here's our final logline:

Pirates of the Caribbean – Curse of the Black Pearl: When the governor's daughter is kidnapped by a band of cursed pirates, her scrupulous lover must join forces with a half-mad pirate captain to save her before she is sacrificed to end the curse.

One more to go. For *How to Train Your Dragon*, we have the boy and the dragon. So, starting with the boy…

- Hapless
- Clumsy
- Misfit
- Wimpy
- Gangly

Actually, I tricked you (so sorry). I'm going to take two of these adjectives and just drop the noun *boy*. The new version will use *clumsy misfit*. Sometimes an adjective can be used as a noun, as you see here. That's a handy trick when you want to get in a little extra description without stringing adjectives behind a poor noun like the chains on Jacob Marley's ghost. Now we'll do the dragon.

- Fearsome
- Smart
- Black
- Cute
- Wounded

Now here's where this gets interesting and really shows the

power of an adjective. Depending on the adjective we pick, we can completely change the story implied in the logline.

We could take *fearsome* and imply that this a story about how the wimpy boy overpowers a scary dragon. Or we could use *cute* and imply that it's just a cuddly dragon baby and not really that much of a threat. We could try *smart*, which makes me think of something like *Air Bud* with dragons. Come to think of it, that'd be pretty cool!

But most appropriate in this case is *wounded*, as it shows that this is a friendship born out of necessity, and it leaves the fearsomeness of the dragon up to the reader to imagine. Our new and improved (now with more adjectives!) logline is:

How to Train Your Dragon: Against the traditions of his Viking tribe, a clumsy misfit befriends a wounded dragon and discovers secrets about the creatures that will change his tribe's way of life forever.

So get out your logline and an adjective feather. See what happens when you tickle your reader's imagination with a decent descriptive word or three.

Exercises

- Take the characters from your favorite stories and make up adjective-noun pairs for them. Use those pairs to logline one or two of those stories.

- Brainstorm a list of adjectives for each important character in your story's logline. Take that list and pick the ones that work the best to show the conflict and irony in your story, then write a logline using them.

Stop Avoiding Conflict

Throughout this book, I've danced around the idea that a good logline contains conflict and irony. I've even given you plenty of examples that contain one or both. But I haven't talked specifically about how each works. It's time now to concentrate on bringing those two elements to your logline party. We'll cover conflict in this chapter, and we'll look at how to use irony in the next one.

Conflict is the fundamental element of story, but it's also an element that is often misunderstood or outright ignored, especially by beginning storytellers. So let's go back to the basics for a minute.

Every story is about somebody (the main character) who wants something (a goal). This goal could be anything, but some of the most popular ones are things like wealth, love, a promotion, love, revenge, and love.

However, for this to be an interesting story (actually, for it to be a story at all), somebody or something must oppose the main character and try to keep him from reaching his goal. That something or somebody is called the antagonist, or the antagonistic force if it's inanimate or internal. That's the source of the conflict.

"But I can write a story without conflict," you protest. "I'm working on one right now. It's a movie called *The Shopping Trip* and it's about a girl who goes to the mall and does some shopping."

Okay. Let's write a logline.

The Shopping Trip: A girl goes to the mall and does some shopping.

Hear that sound?

No?

Come on, don't you hear that distinct sound of silence?

That's the sound of thousands of people *not* jumping out of their seats and running, not walking, to the nearest movie theater to see *The Shopping Trip*.

I hate to break it to you, but nobody ever made a career out of an empty theater. (Except maybe the janitor!)

So what do you do? Well, you find the conflict in your story. What does this girl want? What's keeping her from getting it?

Let's look at a logline for a Hollywood movie before and after we add conflict. Here's one that needs some help in the conflict department:

Tangled: A girl with really long hair fulfills her dream.

Okay, that's not too compelling. What's stopping her from fulfilling her dream? Let's put in some conflict.

Tangled: A girl with really long hair runs away from home to fulfill her dream.

Now we see a little bit of conflict. It doesn't really grab you, but it's a start. This logline isn't going to get the audience into the theater yet, so let's think about how we can make it better by looking at the other sources of conflict.

The movie has a few other conflict points that we can play with. We could work with the type of home the girl runs away from, or we could add something about the guy that she runs away with. Her home situation is rather difficult to get into a piece of a single sentence, so let's be lazy and start with her road companion.

Tangled: A girl with really long hair runs away from home with a handsome thief to fulfill her dream.

That's more interesting, isn't it? But it could be better. Let's go back to the home situation. If we take a cue from one of the film's trailers and boil it down to being grounded for, like, forever, we might get somewhere. We'll have to do a little rewriting to fit it in, but we can do it.

Tangled: A long-haired girl who has been grounded for her entire life runs away with a handsome thief to fulfill her dream.

Now we have two external conflict points with the thief and the grounding. Let's get more specific about her dream, so it's not like defeating a vague darkness within herself. Concrete goals are always best.

Tangled: A long-haired girl who has been grounded for her entire life runs away with a handsome thief to fulfill her dream of seeing the world outside her window.

This could still be better. The movie is really about how the girl's dream changes after she leaves the tower. And that's internal conflict. Bingo! Let's add it to all this external conflict we're talking about. We can rewrite the logline drastically to work in some of the internal conflict.

Tangled: To fulfill her dream of leaving a tower she's lived in for eighteen years, a long-haired girl runs away with a handsome thief and discovers what it means to find a new dream.

That's pretty good. It's a whole lot better than where we started!

For those of you who have seen *Tangled*, you're probably thinking that a lot was left out to make this logline. After all, it's a complicated story! You're right, of course. I did leave a lot out.

Remember, a logline is for sparking interest in your potential audience. You're trying to get down to the essence of the story. You know the rest of the details, so you just need to pique the audience's interest enough to make them want to know more. Let 'em see some good conflict and they'll be begging you to tell them the rest of the story.

Exercises

- Pick out some of your favorite stories and figure out what the conflict is in each, then write a logline for one or two that emphasizes the conflict in the story.

- What is in the way of your protagonist reaching his goal? Find a way to get that into your story's logline and show us the conflict.

How Ironic That We Don't Use Irony

Irony is a valuable commodity in a logline. It makes your audience settle back into their seats thinking, "This is gonna be good!" Everybody loves irony.

What's irony? It's the juxtaposition of two things that don't tend to go together. Kind of like the peanut butter and mayonnaise sandwich that sounds disgusting but somehow is supposed to work. (I've never quite been brave enough to test that one.)

In a story, irony is often putting a character in a situation that he never expected to be in, or it's putting two characters with opposing viewpoints on the same team. It makes us think about how this story is going to show different sides of the same coin.

Audiences love stories that show them two (or more!) sides of a coin. (Though I suppose if it had more than two sides, it wouldn't be a coin, would it?) We enjoy deep movies and books that explore all the little nooks and crannies of a theme.

A theme, by the way, is the main idea that your story is exploring. The stories we consider classics often have several characters who each live out a different facet of a theme, giving the audience a vast experience with an idea and allowing them to see where following that idea would lead.

In comedy, irony is great, because irony can be very funny when done right. The key for loglines is to use irony to hint at the comedy and let the audience run wild thinking about how funny the premise can be.

Whether drama or a comedy, how does irony work in practice? Let's grab some Hollywood films and check it out.

Drama is easy, so let's start there. We can use a logline from some of the previous chapters to illustrate this. The logline from *Jurassic Park* already has some great irony.

Jurassic Park: A kid-hating scientist must protect two children when a dinosaur park goes haywire and the monsters go on rampage.

How ironic! You mean this scientist who hates kids is going to be stuck in a dangerous dinosaur park with two children for a good portion of this movie? Some sparks are going to fly, that's for sure.

Or how about the logline from *Pirates of the Caribbean – Curse of the Black Pearl*?

Pirates of the Caribbean – Curse of the Black Pearl: When the governor's daughter is kidnapped by a band of cursed pirates, her scrupulous lover must join forces with a half-mad pirate captain to save her before she is sacrificed to end the curse.

As I hinted at in the adjective post, this logline has a lot of irony going for it. A scrupulous guy has to join up with a criminal pirate (and a half-mad one at that!) to save his girl from other pirates? How ironic!

Both of these loglines use adjectives to show the irony of the dramatic situation. The audience immediately starts thinking about how interesting this movie will be because of the situation the characters have been thrown into.

Not too hard, is it? Well, we haven't covered funny stories yet, but that's not much harder. With these, we want to use irony to show how hilarious this situation can get. Let's try a movie where the hook is meant to be humorous.

Despicable Me: A super villain must adopt three adorable orphans to carry out his evil plot, bringing chaos to his secret lair and making him wonder if villainy is really all that great.

How do we make this logline ironic? Well, the humor here is that a super villain has to adopt some kids as a key part of his plan. We need to use our logline tricks to bring out the irony. We could start by showing how much this villain hates kids.

Despicable Me: A super villain who delights in making children cry must adopt three adorable orphans as part of his next evil plot, bringing chaos to his secret lair and making him wonder if villainy is really all that great.

That adds some irony, but it could be even more fun if we mention that these kids have to like him! We'll have to rewrite this a lot to make it work.

Despicable Me: A super villain who delights in making children cry must adopt three adorable girls as part of his next scheme, bringing chaos to his secret lair as he tries to keep the kids happy.

Now that's funny! You mean this villain who likes to see kids cry is going to have to keep these girls happy to carry out his plan? How ironic! And we the audience can totally see the girls running wild in his lair, trying out his death rays and villain equipment. This guy has his hands full of an ironic mess, and we can't wait to see what happens next!

As a side note, you'll notice that I eliminated the part about making the villain wonder if his villainy was worthwhile. Part of writing a great logline is making it compellingly promise your premise without misleading the audience. *Despicable Me* was "sold" to me on the premise of the logline we started with, but it didn't deliver on it, ultimately leaving me disappointed in the film. So I chose to write a much more honest logline, even if it wasn't as compelling.

The lesson here is that if you can't write a compelling logline for your story, maybe something's wrong and you need to go back and rework some things! If that's the case, jump in with both feet, remembering that irony is one of the keys to a great story. Rejigger your story into shape, then go write a logline that sends folks running for a theater or bookstore.

Exercises

- Get out your favorite stories again and see if they use irony. Some stories aren't very ironic, but you can often find irony if you look hard enough. Write a logline for one or two and try to emphasize the ironic elements.

- If you can add some irony to your story's logline, write a version to include it.

Do You Ever Feel Set Up?

Sometimes, your story is a little more complicated than our straightforward format. Sometimes, you need to set things up a little more. Enter the setup clause.

You'll recall our second logline template from way back at the beginning of the book.

After something happens to set things up, an adjective protagonist must do something that will set up a climactic encounter with an adjective antagonist/antagonistic force.

The first part, "After something happens...," is the setup clause. Let's look at a logline to get an idea of how it works.

Apollo 13: When a moon mission goes horribly wrong, three astronauts are forced to improvise a new way home.

"When a moon mission goes horribly wrong" is the setup clause. What's it doing for us?

It's showing us something that happened before the main hook of the story. We watch *Apollo 13* to see the astronauts make up a new way to get home. But they can't make up a new way to get home unless there's a reason to do it.

That's what our setup clause does. Because *Apollo 13*'s inciting incident (the mission goes wrong) comes late in the film, the setup clause gets us over the long (but necessary) introduction and into the reason we're watching.

Here's another example:

Thor: After he is banished from his home world, an impulsive titan must fit in on Earth and save it from his conniving brother's plot.

We watch the movie to see Thor bumble around on Earth and duke it out with Loki at the end. But the film takes between twenty and thirty minutes to actually get to the point of Thor trying to fit in as a human. To manage the audience's expectations, Thor's logline requires a setup clause.

You can also use a setup clause to include information that isn't in the story, but is important to help you get started. Like this one from a participant in one of my logline workshop threads on an online forum:

Captured: Stuck in a make-shift prison where he's already made all the other prisoners angry, a cantankerous gnome must work together with the infuriated captives to escape or risk staying imprisoned for the rest of his life.

Though I haven't read this story, the setup clause lets me know that the gnome is already in the prison at the start of the story. This is a starting condition that is essential to understanding the hook, but the story doesn't cover the details of how the condition was obtained.

Now, here's a caveat that's actually a powerful tool. Sometimes a story that needs a setup clause to succeed in a logline is actually in a bad state of disrepair. Let me share a really bad logline from my past.

The Portal: Stumbling on a portal and fleeing through it to escape trouble at home, a rebellious teen is forced to return and reconcile with his family to obtain the one item he needs to capture a crime lord from a parallel universe.

First of all, that logline is way too long. But more importantly, the setup clause points out a big story problem that's not readily obvious unless you've read the screenplay. It's simple: The story isn't about the rebellious teen.

When I was working on this story, my co-writer and I were convinced that the screenplay had to start with the rebellious teen. He was the most interesting character and he had the furthest to go in terms of character arc, so we assumed he was the main character.

There was just one problem. About ten pages into the script, he disappears and is replaced as the main character by three kids who find his portal and start the real story. A better logline for the script would have been something like this:

The Portal: When three kids find a portal to another dimension and release a vengeful crime lord, they must join forces with the portal's rebellious creator to set things right.

That's still not all that great, but hey, the script needs a lot of work! And that's the point here. By writing a logline for the story, I realized exactly what was wrong. The script was trying to focus on the wrong character. Whoops!

How cool is that? I mean besides the fact that now I'm stuck with a broken script that I should have loglined before writing. But maybe I'll fix it someday.

Do you have a story that needs some setup? Perfect. You now have the power of the setup clause to really make your logline shine.

Exercises

- Try to logline one of your favorite stories that requires a setup clause.

- Check your story's logline and see if it could benefit from a setup clause. If so, rewrite it to include one.

What Makes Your Story Different?

One of the key questions that you need to answer with your logline is this: What makes this story different?

You can write a brilliant logline, but if it sounds the same as other stories in the same genre, you're going to have problems picking up an audience. So what do you do? Simple. Focus on what's different about your story and play it up.

Let's take a look at two of the most tired storylines out there. We'll start with the romantic comedy. You know the formula. Boy meets girl (or girl meets boy), boy falls in love with girl (or vice versa), girl can't stand boy (or vice versa), a matchmaker or circumstances hilariously shove boy and girl together, and voilá! Boy and girl get married. (In an ideal story anyway!)

Here's a tired-concept logline for a romantic comedy:

I.Q.: An average-intelligence mechanic falls for a brilliant mathematics student and tries to win her from her stuffy suitor.

Ho hum. Wake me up when it's over. Zzzzzzzz...

But wait! This movie is actually pretty good! Why? Because it has a really funny hook: Albert Einstein is the girl's uncle, and he's the matchmaker character in this movie.

Zzzzz...HmWhat?! Hey, that's interesting! How do we logline that?

I.Q.: When an average-intelligence mechanic falls for the niece of Albert Einstein, his only chance of winning her heart is to pretend to be a brainiac with her uncle's help.

Now we've got something. How many romantic comedies besides this one have Albert Einstein? Zero! This movie is different from anything else out there, and it's crazy enough that it might even pull in people who don't like the genre!

Another tired storyline is the one where the pet gets separated from its person and must brave the world to get home again. Like this one:

Bolt: After he gets lost in New York, a dog must cross the continent to get back home to California.

Wait, I think I've seen this one. No? This is different?

It is, actually. The dog thinks he's a superhero and has no idea what to do with the real world. So we can logline it like this:

Bolt: After he is mistakenly shipped to New York, a TV star dog who thinks he's a superhero must survive the real world to get back to his owner in Hollywood.

I'll see that one!

You can see how finding your unique hook and playing it up in your logline can do wonders for increasing the appeal of your story. By looking at what makes your story unique, you can often find the best way to logline it.

Exercises

- Pick a story you like and try to logline it based on what makes it unique.

- Find what's unique about your story and write your logline to highlight it.

Leave the Moral Out of This!

One common logline problem that I bump into every now and then, especially in the faith-based storytelling circles I hang out in, is the tendency to put the moral of the story into the logline. This, however, is usually one of the worst things you could do.

When we pick up a fictional book or movie, we're not interested in what we're going to learn. Instead, we're interested in what the story is about.

Now, we might like to have an idea of the kind of "lesson" we might find in this story, but we're all kind of stubborn people. For some reason, we don't want to know what we're supposed to learn. In fact, if we know what we're supposed to learn, we'll sometimes go to great lengths to avoid it.

We're kind of silly, aren't we?

But regardless, that's the way we work. And so when we write our loglines, we want to stay away from putting the moral in the logline. Or do we?

What if we could imply the moral so that it tickles that part of us that wants an inkling of the "lesson" of the story, without going so far with it that we tell it outright and annoy the part that doesn't want to know what the moral actually is?

We can! But first we have to talk about theme.

I've tossed around the idea of theme here and there throughout this book, but I haven't really launched into a definition of it. That's because it's tough to nail down what a theme actually is. I'll try, though. For your sake.

Let's start with what a theme is not. Contrary to the beliefs of some, the theme is not the moral of the story. It's a question that will be explored in the story.

I know, it's tough to grasp what that actually is. I told you that this was hard to define! But if we explore the concept of theme a little more, you'll get the idea, I think.

In more academic storytelling circles, the moral of a story is sometimes known as a *thesis*. That should call something to your mind. In fact, it might make you want to hide under a rock, because a thesis is something we all remember from (brace yourself) essay writing. (Can't say I didn't warn you. Now quit screaming and get back over here. It's not that bad.)

Sorry to scare you like that. But it's a great way to remember the difference. A thesis is a statement of a position on a topic. Something like these:

- We should sacrifice what's comfortable for what's right.

- Guys should open doors for girls.

- People should pronounce the word "milk" correctly. (I'm serious! This was a real thesis that I once heard somebody give in a brainstorming session!)

But if we were to talk about each thesis from that list in terms of theme, we'd have this:

- Sacrifice

- Chivalry

- Proper Pronunciation

See the difference? Simply put, a theme is a topic, and a thesis is a conclusion from the exploration of that topic. This is why we talk about how a story explored a theme, but we never say, "Wow, that story explored the thesis so well!"

Armed with this information, we can get the theme into the logline. The goal here is to compellingly portray the situation in the story, evoking a theme, and making people wonder what thesis will be found at the end.

Here's the logline from *Tangled* that we wrote back in the chapter on conflict:

Tangled: To fulfill her dream of leaving a tower she's lived in for eighteen years, a long-haired girl runs away with a handsome thief and discovers what it means to find a new dream.

You see how we've mentioned what this girl will discover in the course of the film, but we haven't told the outcome. You could still go either way with this. She could discover that dreams are better left undreamt, or she could find out that it's wonderful to dream. Or even both, if the ending is a bittersweet one.

Let's do one from start to finish to see how this can work. Here's a version with the moral in the logline.

Wall-E: When a lonely robot tasked with clean-up duty on an abandoned Earth falls in love with a probe, he chases her back to the humans' ship, proving that true love overcomes any boundary.

Okay, so I've told you what you're going to learn. It's like one of those really lame movie trailers where they give away the ending.

Don't you hate those?

We really have a fairly decent logline without the moral, so let's pull that out and see how it sits.

Wall-E: When a lonely robot tasked with clean-up duty on an abandoned Earth falls in love with a probe, he chases her back to the humans' ship.

That version ends too early. We need something to imply the conflict and theme. Actually, we've already implied the theme by writing a logline about robots that fall in love. So we just need some conflict on the end and we'll be done!

Wall-E: When a lonely robot tasked with clean-up duty on an abandoned Earth falls in love with a probe, he chases her back to the humans' ship to try to win her affections.

Although everybody knows that the movie involves so much more than that, the film really boils down to the gist of the logline above. Wall-E chases Eve around the huge spaceship, causing problems while he tries to get a response from her.

So now we have conflict and theme, and a decent logline. And now you see how this works. Go on, now. You can do this too! Don't let me catch you with a moral in your logline again!

Exercises

- Find the morals in some of your favorite stories, then try writing a logline for one or two of those stories with the theme in mind.

- Is there a moral in your story's logline? Rewrite to focus on the theme instead of the thesis.

The Handy-Dandy Three-Sentence Trick

Every now and then, you find that your story just won't cooperate when it comes to writing a logline. You try untangling the threads, but you don't get anywhere. You use all the tricks you've read in this book, but you just can't seem to find the angle that works.

Worse still, the thought of cramming your story into just one sentence becomes daunting. You can't possibly do this, can you? Come on, one sentence?!?

When I see somebody with this problem, I reach into my back pocket and whip out... (drumroll, please) The Handy-Dandy Three-Sentence Trick!

What I think happens is that the logline becomes intimidating. A single sentence feels ever so impossible when you're writing a 100,000-word novel or a 2-hour movie, doesn't it? Your brain rebels and shuts down. It even begins to tell you that there's no good reason to write a logline.

So here's what you do: You trick your brain.

That's right. Tell yourself that you have *three* sentences to tell about your story. After you've been trying to squish it all into one, three is a luxury! Suddenly, it's easy.

Take it further, though. Set no limits on which story threads to include. Don't try to keep it to the main threads. Just write three sentences to create a summary-type paragraph. What's your story about? Go.

Here's what I came up with for the movie *Waking Ned Devine*:

After their neighbor wins the lottery and dies of shock, two men from a small Irish village try to rally the town to pretend he's still alive so they can claim and split the prize money. Meanwhile, a poor pig farmer tries to win the heart of a local girl ahead of an upstaging rival. As the lottery judge arrives and the village crank tries to bargain for a bigger share of the pot, pulling off the con becomes more and more impossible.

After all these loglines, that sure seems like a lot, doesn't it? You're right! Now that you're used to thinking in single-sentence loglines, you can look through this ginormous sea of three sentences and spot the interesting parts. You can notice what would be unnecessary or excessive to put in a logline, then take your conclusions and rewrite into one sentence. Let's break this one down.

We have three stories in here, it looks like. There's the story of scheming to collect the prize money, the romance subplot, and the plot with the village crank. The last of those ties into the first storyline, but it's somewhat separate.

Now we start to pull things from our sentences that we like. What in here will make a good logline?

Because two out of three of our threads focus on trying to con the lottery judge, let's start by deciding to leave out the love story subplot. While that's an interesting thread too, it's not what the main story thread is about.

Let's take the two remaining pieces from our three-sentence summary and write a logline playing to those plots:

Waking Ned Devine: After a man from a small Irish village wins the lottery and dies of shock, two old rogues try to convince the rest of the village to pretend he's still alive so they can split the prize money—but they run into trouble when the village crank demands a larger share.

This is heading in the right direction, but we're not quite there yet. Even though the storyline with the village crank is related to the main thread and is interesting, including it here just makes a compelling logline overly long. We don't really need it here. Two guys try to get an entire village to pretend a dead man is still alive so they can collect his prize money. That's all we need to get the entire concept.

With that in mind, let's simplify by removing the village crank (that'll make her mad, I'll bet), which gives us this logline:

Waking Ned Devine: After a man from a small Irish village wins the lottery and dies of shock, two old rogues try to convince the rest of the village to pretend he's still alive so they can split the prize money.

That worked out nicely!

Okay, but what if you can't find the common story thread from your three sentences? That would be an issue, wouldn't it?

First of all, rest assured that it's there if you have a story. You can't not have a main thread, even if you can't find it. But you *can* be too close to your story to see it.

In this case, one thing you can do is ask a few people to look at your sentences and tell you which parts jump out at them. Which parts make them want to know how this turns out? Take that feedback and write your logline to play toward the threads that resonate best with your test audience. You might even discover that your story needs to be reworked to hit those beats a little harder.

So now you know what to do when that single sentence has you down. Give yourself three sentences, fool your brain, and you'll have a logline in no time!

Exercises

- Give the three-sentence trick a try with one of your favorite stories.

- Use the three-sentence trick to logline one of your own stories.

Characters Deserve Loglines Too

Ever have one of those days when your characters are being demanding? You know the type. They keep yelling at you about things they want.

"I wouldn't have done that. Rewrite it."

"Why'd you kill my true love?"

"I want my own logline!"

Wait, that last one is news to you? Your characters don't say that?

Well. Let me talk to them a second. Hey characters! You should all demand your own loglines!

Oh, now you're mad at me for getting them started again. Sorry. Let's escape to a soundproof room and we'll talk about how to placate them.

Wow. Look at that angry mob of characters. Maybe we'd better think about giving them each their own logline. Come to think of it, this might be a win-win situation!

You remember back when we loglined *Pirates of the Caribbean*? One of the hardest parts of loglining that film was that are so many characters to think about. Who is the main character?

Who carries the story? What story do we play to in the logline?

What if we wrote a logline for each character to see how the story looks from each perspective?

It's worth thinking about. Not only would we be able to look at each story thread in a logline form, we'd also get a way to see each character's goal. That sounds pretty good to me! Let's give it a whirl.

First let's make a list of some characters in *Pirates of the Caribbean.*

- Jack Sparrow

- Will Turner

- Elizabeth Swann

- Norrington

- Barbossa

Now let's write a logline for each one. This is a little bit different from the way you'd write a logline for your story. Here, you're writing from the character's perspective. Don't consider what the audience knows about the story, but stick strictly to the character's sphere of reference.

Let's go down the line so you can see how this works.

Jack: After he is caught trying to steal a ship, a half-mad pirate captain is broken out of prison to help rescue the governor's daughter from his old crew—the crew that mutinied against him.

We're writing from Jack's perspective. His enemy is his old crew that he's got a score to settle with. He'd like to get a ship. But does he know anything about Will and Elizabeth's relationship? Not beyond the fact that it exists, really.

Will: After his true love is kidnapped by pirates, a scrupulous young blacksmith must enlist the help of a half-mad pirate captain to chase down the rogues.

Again, we're working from the character's perspective. Will doesn't know all the details about Jack and his mutinous old crew, so that stays out of the logline. All he knows is that he needs to rescue his girl and the only way to do that is to join forces with Jack.

Elizabeth: When she is kidnapped by a band of cursed pirates, the governor's daughter must survive until she is rescued from being sacrificed to end a curse.

Here's where this whole character's perspective thing gets really interesting. Elizabeth doesn't know that anybody's coming after her. All she knows is that the creepy pirates have kidnapped her and she needs to stay alive.

Norrington: A British captain gets his chance to upstage his rival for the hand of the governor's daughter when she is kidnapped by pirates.

And now things get even more interesting because now we're writing a logline for one of the bad guys. This is incredibly useful, giving us a clear statement of his motivation and goal.

Barbossa: A cursed pirate captain must kidnap the governor's daughter and evade capture to end the curse on himself and his crew.

Like Norrington's logline, here we have the bad guy's goal clearly stated. It gives us something to hold on to while we're writing him. We can refer back to either bad guy's logline and make sure he is doing things consistently with his goal.

If that wasn't cool enough, we can now use this information to help us write a logline for the story. We can look at the storylines for each of our three heroes and find the one who's the most active as a starting point. If we check our loglines for Jack, Will, and Elizabeth, we'll quickly notice that Will is the one doing the most. And if you remember the logline from the earlier chapter, you'll recall that we used Will as the main character when we wrote this logline:

Pirates of the Caribbean – Curse of the Black Pearl: When the governor's daughter is kidnapped by a band of cursed pirates, her scrupulous lover must join forces with a half-mad pirate captain to save her before she is sacrificed to end the curse.

But just because we've decided to use Will to logline the story doesn't mean we should throw out those other loglines! In fact, you should definitely save the loglines you wrote for each of your characters.

Why?

Because you can use them to keep those characters on track. Your characters' loglines tell you what they want, something about how they expect to get it, and how they got into the mess they're in now. That's valuable information!

You can use that information to check your characters' behavior and make sure they're living up to their loglines. (Now there's a neat thought.) It's not necessarily something you need to do constantly, but you might re-read your character loglines after you finish a draft. That can go a long way toward helping you pinpoint problems with character motivation when you're scouting for things to fix in future drafts.

So. Let's go on out there where your characters are still rioting and tell them what we've come up with. With any luck, they'll accept our terms without demanding too much of a pay raise.

Exercises

- Pick one of your favorite stories with a decent-sized cast of characters (three or four is great, six or seven is fantastic) and write a logline for each.

- Write a logline for each of the characters in your story. Bonus points if you use your loglines to check on your characters' motivation after you finish the next draft.

In a World Where...

We've talked a lot about loglines and story. Story story story. And while story is indeed important, sometimes you have to pitch from another angle. Sometimes, even when you have a great story, your hook is something else.

For instance, let's say you've got a really cool alternate history realm to tell your story in. Cool! That's almost intriguing enough to be the hook all by itself. But not quite.

Or perhaps you have a story about a robot. Wow! How are you going to portray human emotion with that character? I'm intrigued, but I need to see the story.

So what do you do? You need to get both the hook and the story into the logline. But how can you give your audience a glimpse at the unique hook of your story without losing the story itself?

Let's take those two examples one by one. We'll start with the alternate history idea.

When you have a unique story world like alternate history, the hardest part is that all the rules for your world that you've come up with are too complicated for a logline. You may protest and say that you can explain them quickly, but trust me, you're going to want to focus on the core story and let the interested reader discover the rules for himself. But you can hint at those things just a little bit.

What you don't want to do is dump information about your story world's rules and regulations on your reader. This is one of the most common mistakes I see when helping somebody with a unique world write a logline: they get bogged down in talking about the rules.

Remember that your story is the most important part of your pitch. A cool setting is a nice hook, but it doesn't compare with a great story.

Let me give you a great example. Author Aubrey Hansen has a book called *Peter's Angel* that just so happens to be an alternate history novel. I had the privilege of helping her logline it, and she's agreed to let me share that logline with you.

When she told me *Peter's Angel* was an alternate history novel, I was immediately intrigued and told her that she needed to get that into her pitch. What we ended up with was a logline for her series that looks like this:

The Peter's Angel Saga: In an alternate world where America lost the War for Independence, a patriot colonel accidentally uncovers an exiled British duke and rebels against England in an attempt to restore the nobleman to his throne.

Yes, I said this is the logline for her *series*. We'll talk about that in the next chapter, okay? For now, let's just look at how this breaks down.

First of all, notice that we've taken a setup clause and repurposed it. Instead of telling the audience something that happens at the beginning of the story, we're using it to give some backstory and background on the story world. This one sets up the whole concept of Aubrey's alternate history hook: America lost the Revolution.

So now we're intrigued, but we need some story to really make us grab the book and read it. Easy, right? By now you know how the story part of the logline works. That part is nice and straightforward.

But there's a little bit here that gives us just a tiny glimpse into how the world of *Peter's Angel* works. She's told us that the main character is a "patriot colonel" in this America-lost-the-Revolution alternate world. And she's let us know that there are British dukes in this world, so we gather there's some form of aristocracy here.

This is huge. We've gotten a whole bunch of little tidbits in the subtleties of this logline, all without becoming bogged down or overwhelmed with countless details. We know just enough to want to delve into this world. And that's exactly the way it should be.

Okay, now let's turn to the other example, the one where our hook is an interesting main character. You know, like if your main character is a robot with human emotions. Yes, I'm going to pull out *Wall-E* again. It's a great movie.

With *Wall-E*, then, the biggest deal with getting somebody interested in this story is that a robot is the main character. I've talked to many people who haven't seen the film, and almost all of them wonder out loud about why I like a movie about a robot so much.

Then they see the movie and love it, but that's with my enthusiastic and annoying you-must-see-this-movie act. What if they just see a logline somewhere? It's going to have to convince them without me being there to bounce excitedly about the prospect of showing *Wall-E* to another friend.

In an earlier chapter, I showed you this logline:

Wall-E: When a lonely robot tasked with clean-up duty on an abandoned Earth falls in love with a probe, he chases her back to the humans' ship to try to win her affections.

That's how you logline a robot main character. You humanize the robot and let us know that it can emote. Let's break this down.

First, we've used the word lonely as our adjective, ascribing human emotions to the machine. That's interesting, so we keep reading. Now we come to "falls in love" and that's intriguing, so we keep going. Finally, we find a robot that somehow got human emotions trying to teach another robot to have those same emotions.

I'll take a ticket for the front row, please.

You can apply these techniques to almost any unique concept you have. That setup clause we used for Peter's Angel is a pretty versatile thing, and you can use it for all sorts of story worlds or concepts. The main thing is to remember that your expansive story world is too big to detail in a logline, so stick to the main hook.

And with our *Wall-E* example, you can see how you can pitch almost any story by playing the logline to emotion. The possibilities are pretty much endless, as long as you remember that story is king. Keep the setting as a neat backdrop that gets us interested and keep the characters as the players in the story, and we'll come along gladly to experience the tale you have to tell.

Exercises

- Make a list of some stories you're familiar with that could include an element other than story in the pitch. Try loglining a few of them.

- Do you have a story that could benefit from adding setting or characters to the pitch? If you do, give it a try.

Finding the Core of Your Series

Now that we've gone through all sorts of theory for loglining a solitary story, I think it's time we answer the guy way in the back who's been patiently holding his hand up for all this time. What's your question, friend?

What's that? Oh! Can you write a logline for a series?

Of course you can. And it's a great idea to consider.

Think about this... If you have a series of books, or maybe a TV show or web series you're trying to pitch, you'll want to sell it as a whole. You'll want a logline for each installment, but you're going to have to explain what the whole thing is about. A perfect place for a logline!

Before we can start loglining your series, we need to talk about the two types of series. They behave in different ways and require quite different approaches to loglining, so let's take a look.

The first kind is the Serial series (redundancy, woot!). You have an overarching story that carries through the entire series. In the first installment, you set things up that don't get taken care of until the series is ended. In terms of stories you might be familiar with, think of *The Lord of the Rings* or *The Hunger Games*.

Then there's the second kind, the Continuing Adventures series. There isn't an overarching story and the characters are the focus. Each installment has closure at its end point. This would be stories like *Star Trek* or *Indiana Jones*, or perhaps your favorite TV sitcom.

So, now that we have a definition of the two types of series, let's look at how you'd write a logline for each kind. We'll start with the Continuing Adventures series, since the last shall be first. Besides, it's easier.

With a Continuing Adventures series, you're concerned with the characters and setting. You want to get people excited about following a character on his adventures. For example, if we logline *Star Trek*, we get something like this:

Star Trek: The adventures of the crew of a starship as they explore the far reaches of the universe.

Now, with this kind of series, you'll most definitely want to have the next logline ready. That's because you've just fed your prospective audience a setting, not a story. They may perk up at the setting ("Ooh! Spaceship!"), but if you don't give them a story quickly, they'll find another neat setting to gaze upon.

Now let's turn our attention to the Serial type of series. Because there's an overarching story here, you're going to want to give us more of a regular logline. This is a little bit more difficult.

Here's the deal... Remember when we talked about untangling all the threads of your story and finding the main one? That's what's going on here, only now you've got a bunch of installments to think about, and all the threads in each of those stories to boot. Pretty intimidating.

But it's not too bad. This is very much the same concept as before. Figure out what happens in each installment, then figure out the big, overarching through-line. Where are you going with your story on a series level?

This is easier to see with an example, so let's go back to the logline that I helped author Aubrey Hansen write for her *Peter's Angel* trilogy.

The Peter's Angel Saga: In an alternate world where America lost the War for Independence, a patriot colonel accidentally uncovers an exiled British duke and rebels against England in an attempt to restore the nobleman to his throne.

Looks like a logline for just one story, doesn't it? That's the idea. You should know your character's big-picture goal for the entire series, the main thread of the series-wide story, and play to that in your series logline. Then you can drill down with each individual book's logline and talk about what happens in just that one installment.

So you can see how this works in practice, here's the logline for the first book in *The Peter's Angel Saga* that Aubrey gives to people after she tells them about the series as a whole:

Peter's Angel: After he is saved from certain death at the hands of kidnappers, a young patriot colonel determines to find the mysterious boy who rescued him. But his rescuer has a deadly secret of his own and will do anything to keep from being found.

"Wait! Hold it!" you shout. "Aubrey broke one of the logline rules! Didn't you say loglines should be only a single sentence?"

I did.

Here's why she can get away with this. She's already got you asking for more with that logline for the series. Because of that, this is more like if she'd given you a logline for the first book, then you asked for more and she's giving you more details.

Now, of course, she should also have a single-sentence logline for each book, but I was showing you her pitching process, not her logline. And yes, you should plan out how you'll be pitching. More on that in the next chapter.

Would you like to see another way you can break a logline rule that's related to loglining a series? Yes?

You're rebellious, aren't you? But okay.

This whole series thing gets really interesting when you start talking about the further installments. After all, if your audience has (ideally) seen/read your first story, it stands to reason that they don't need much convincing to come back for the sequel.

You'd think that, and in some ways it's true. But you still need to pull them in or they won't come. There's one extra luxury, though. If you've already set up the characters and your audience knows who they are, you can name names.

For example, if you wanted to logline the movie *Back to the Future Part 2*, you might do something like this:

Back to the Future Part 2: After Biff steals the time machine and creates a nightmarish alternate future where he rules Marty's hometown, Marty and Doc must travel back in time and stop him.

Anyone who wants to see this movie will have already seen *Back to the Future*, so we can call Biff, Marty, and Doc by name. The potential audience for this film knows exactly who they are, and the sequel actually isn't all that compelling with our usual adjective-noun pairings. I mean, look at this:

Back to the Future Part 2: After the school bully steals the time machine and creates a nightmarish alternate future where he rules a regular high school kid's hometown, the kid and the scientist who built the machine must travel back in time and stop him.

That's not going to work! And why would we bother trying to fix that convoluted mess when we're allowed to use the character names now? We don't need to, because we can name names in sequel loglines.

With one caveat, that is. If your series is of the Continuing Adventures sort, I recommend that you have a conventional, rule-following logline for each installment. People can and will come into that type of series anywhere, so you're going to want to make sure you can grab them no matter which installment they pick up first.

But what if, as often happens nowadays, you have an Continuing Adventures series with a few installments that feel more like a Serial series?

The first thing to remember is that it's still a Continuing Adventures series. It still fits under the umbrella of your main series logline, and as long as nobody tries to begin with part 2, they should be able understand everything.

Remember, though, that every installment should have its own logline. So in the case of a multi-part storyline, you would have an additional logline. Now you have one logline for the series as a whole, one for the multi-part storyline, and then one for each installment of that storyline.

Here's an example from *Star Trek: The Next Generation*. First, we need a logline for the show itself. It's a Continuing Adventures series, so we'll keep it generic to include a multitude of potential storylines.

Star Trek: The Next Generation: The adventures of the crew of a starship as they explore the far reaches of the universe.

(Yes, it's the same logline as the original *Star Trek*. Both shows had the same premise.)

Next, we'll write a logline for the two-part episode *Time's Arrow*. Remember, because we've already created a logline for the series, we can use character names in the episode loglines.

Time's Arrow: When the crew of the *Enterprise* discovers an ancient version of Data's head buried in the past, they uncover and must stop an alien plot to infiltrate the 19th century.

(Data is an android, by the way, so don't freak out at this logline about him losing his head.)

And finally, here are loglines for each part in the *Time's Arrow* storyline:

Time's Arrow, part 1: When the crew of the *Enterprise* discovers an ancient version of Data's head buried in the past, they investigate and find an alien time portal that Data accidentally stumbles through, trapping him in the 19th century.

Time's Arrow, part 2: After Data is trapped in the 19th century, the crew of the *Enterprise* must find a way to rescue him and overcome an alien plot to infiltrate Earth.

See? Very simple. Just pretend you have a Serial series for the longer storyline and write loglines accordingly.

And there you are. Now you can go forth and logline your series with confidence.

Exercises

- Classify a few of your favorite series into either Serial or Continuing Adventures series types, then write a logline for some of them.

- If you're writing a series, figure out which type it is and logline it. Bonus points if you logline the future installments in light of the first one.

I Wrote a Logline... Now What?

You've read through this whole book. You've taken your logline skills to the next level and learned all sorts of new tricks and tools you can use to compellingly explain in just one sentence what makes your story tick.

But what do you do with the little single-sentence wonder that you've been meticulously crafting for all these pages?

To start with, a logline is a tool for pitching your story to people you need to interest. Producers, agents, publishers, illustrators, and so on. But you can do more than just pitch your story with it. Here are some ideas.

Refine It

Just because you've finished this book and written a logline you love doesn't mean your logline is perfect. Try it out on some people and see how they react.

Not just any people, though. You want to try your logline on many different kinds of folks. Don't just ask your family what they think of it.

Who do you ask? Start with anyone who's been privileged to read a draft of your story. These people know what your story is about and they will be able to tell you right away if you've strayed in your logline. If you've gone off track, back up and refine the logline. Or, if the logline is more compelling than your story, you might even think about rewriting the story. That sounds drastic, but sometimes you realize exactly what your story was missing when you logline it.

Once you have a good logline that passes inspection, move on to people who don't know your story. If you participate in any online writing forums, this is simple: just post your logline! See what people think. If they jump up and down (in an online, text-and-smilies fashion) and beg to read your book, you might just have a winner. Even better is that you just got all those people interested and probably generated some new fans. Make sure your website link is in your signature!

Memorize It

Yep. Memorize it. That way, when someone asks you what you're working on, you can rattle it off without thinking twice. Practice in front of a mirror and be sure to smile big at the end. Okay, maybe not. Depends on how well you smile. (Ask a really good friend for help with that one.)

This is actually pretty important. Until you stop to think about it, you don't realize how many random people ask you what you've been up to. It's not just your friends, either. In fact, you wish it was, because they'll usually listen to you ramble about your story.

Problem is, the question almost always comes from your acquaintances with only a polite interest in your life in general (like that aunt you only see once a year). They want you to give them the gist of your story really fast. Like, I-only-asked-because-I'm-being-polite-so-tell-me-before-my-face-gets-tired-of-smiling-are-you-done-talking-yet-because-I'm-tired-of-listening-to-you-ramble type of fast.

Perfect time to whip out the logline. And then if they ask for more after you throw 'em your clever single-sentence fishing line... Unleash the rambling and reel 'em in!

Actually, it'd be better if you didn't ramble even after you have 'em hooked. That's why you'll want to...

Plan and Practice Your Pitch With It

I know, alliteration. Ain't I cute?

I just said you could unleash the rambling once you had people interested. But you'll get far better results if you know where you're going with your pitch.

This is a matter of trying out your logline that looks ever so nice there on your computer screen, but might not roll off your tongue when you say it. Tweak your masterpiece so you can say it aloud effortlessly, which also helps with memorizing it.

You can cheat when you do this, by the way. I know that I've been telling you for this entire book that a logline is one sentence only. When you pitch out-loud, you can bend that rule a little bit.

Put that sheet of paper away! I didn't mean you get fifteen sentences! No, you don't get a 3x5 card either. Go for two sentences, or at most three. Two and a half, maybe. (And my apologies and sympathy to anyone whose handwriting might require a full sheet of paper for two sentences. Like me.)

You might discover that it helps you to roll into your logline with the story's title. For example, if I were to pitch my screenplay *Bellwether* to you verbally, I might say something like, "*Bellwether* is a feature film about a newbie pastor who gets into unexpected trouble with the domineering church board when he and his wife decide to adopt a child."

And then when they ask for more, what do you do? Well, you should probably have something planned to follow that up. This could be the copy that you're going to write in a little bit (Hey look, a free preview of the next section!), or you could decide to tailor your pitch especially to your specific audience.

So when I give somebody my *Bellwether* logline and they ask for more, I tell them about the pastor's struggles with the church board and how he will ultimately take a stand for truth as he learns about shepherding his flock. That's kind of like my back cover copy, though not quite, because *Bellwether* is a screenplay.

If you decide to tailor your pitch to your audience, you'll want to keep in mind the unique interests of the person or people you're addressing. For example, if you've written a fantasy novel and you're interviewed on a podcast aimed at fantasy fans, play up the fantasy angle! Give them your logline, then tell them why your book is a great fantasy. Dragons, magic, quests, all that cool fantasy stuff. If it's in your story, bring it out.

And it's perfectly acceptable to go with both methods. You can have a general, back-cover blurb follow-up, and you can also make a special follow-up for specific situations. This is my recommended method. Don't forget to save every unique pitch you work out. You might be able to borrow or modify one for a later pitch, and that'll save you some time so you can get back to storytelling.

Write Copy With It

Somehow, people are going to read copy about your story. Whether it's the blurb on the back of the DVD cover, the product description on Amazon, or the little paragraph on the snazzy bookmarks you had printed, you'll be writing some kind of copy somewhere.

But have you ever read the back of a book and thought it sounded intriguing, but then opened the book and found out halfway through that the person who wrote that back copy had no clue what the book was about? Me too. It's terrible.

Don't do that to your story. Use your logline to check the copy, or perhaps even expand your logline into a few more sentences to *be* the copy. Either way, check your copy against your logline and make sure you're still selling on that single sentence.

Check Your Tagline With It

Taglines are those ultra-short sentences that you sometimes find on a book cover or a movie poster. They're also one of my pet peeves. I have a very painful memory about a book that had a little tagline on the front cover: "All he wanted was to go home."

I honestly don't remember a thing about the book beyond the fact that this tagline was completely wrong. That's the negative power of a terrible tagline.

But you don't have to do that because you have your logline! Check your tagline against your logline and make sure that the little bit on your cover or poster actually works with your selling point.

Those are just a few ideas. I'm sure you can think of all sorts of other creative ways to put your logline to work for you.

And with that, you're done with this book, unless you're one of those nice people who likes to read the acknowledgments. May you never be at a loss for a logline!

Exercises

- Take one of your favorite stories that you've loglined in a previous exercise. Use the logline to work out how you might pitch it if it was your own story.

- Use your own story's logline to walk through the ideas in this chapter and get ready to share it with the world.

Jordan Smith

Acknowledgements

This book would not have been possible without the help of the storytellers over at ChristianFilmmakers.org and HolyWorlds.org. The former forum was where I learned how to write loglines in the first place, and I've spent considerable time on both sites helping people with their loglines and testing my theories in the process. Thanks to all of you for being my Guinea pigs!

And while I'm thinking of Holy Worlds, thank you, Lawrence Mark Coddington, for letting me borrow your logline for the chapter on the setup clause.

I've also gotta give a shout-out to the late Blake Snyder, whose chapter on loglines in *Save the Cat! Strikes Back* is valuable and interesting. Your story sense is sorely missed, sir.

I would be remiss if I didn't mention Owl City, Michael Giacchino, and Carolyn Arends, who collectively made up the bulk of the soundtrack of my writing times on this book. Thanks for making music that makes me write better.

Special thanks go out to people who took this book for a test drive and either helped me improve it or just told me that it was good: Jeffrey French, Aubrey Hansen, J. Grace Pennington, Sarah Shafer, Sonya Shafer, and Ben Smith. You guys rock!

Aubrey Hansen and J. Grace Pennington also get some additional thanks for being my test subjects for the concept of loglining a series. Thank you both for hanging out with me on Skype chat and letting me use your stories as Guinea pigs while I figured out how that whole thing worked. Aubrey was also nice enough to let me use her *Peter's Angel* loglines in a couple of chapters. Thanks a bunch!

I'll also give Ben Smith some extra points, and maybe even a level up, for alerting me to the possibility of writing loglines for characters.

More special thanks go to my dad, Doug Smith, who suggested the idea of this revised and expanded edition and got me motivated to get writing.

A big thank you goes to John Shafer for his amazing cover design work. You visualized my title so well.

Extra special thanks go to Ruth Shafer, who edited my book and made it ever so much better. This book wouldn't be nearly as good without your help.

Who Wrote This Book, Anyways?

You're still here? You want to know about me?

I'm honored.

I'm Jordan. Jordan Smith, to be precise. I'm ultimately a story geek, but I tend to be best at expressing that through filmmaking. I'm always picking stories apart to see what makes them tick.

When I'm not thinking about telling stories, I'm usually relaxing with a good book, watching the Detroit Red Wings play hockey, talking to myself in a most alarmingly vast array of voices, or attempting to paralyze my tongue with hot sauce.

If you're still interested in finding out more about me, you can find me blogging at FixMyStory.com. Or, if you're a Twitter type, you can follow @Malfhok and catch up on my 140-character thoughts.

Made in the USA
Middletown, DE
20 November 2018